Box Turtle

Box turtle care, health, diet, breeding, cages, pro's and cons and lots more included

Ben George Carre

Table of Contents

Introduction

Greetings from the exciting world of Box Turtle friendship! This thorough book will assist you in understanding the nuances of taking care of these amazing reptiles, which make for unusual and fulfilling pets. Whether you're a novice pet owner or a seasoned reptile lover, establishing a happy and healthy environment for your box turtle requires an understanding of its care requirements.

We'll explore many facets of caring for box turtles in this tutorial, beginning with the important choice of designing the ideal home. Discover how to create a comfortable and natural-looking house that will provide your box turtle all the things it needs to thrive.

Examine the nutritional requirements of box turtles and determine the ideal ratio of nutrients to maintain their vigor and vitality. We'll also go over typical health concerns and ways to stay healthy in advance, so you can take charge of your shelled companion's care.

It's gratifying to develop a relationship with your box turtle, and we'll provide tips on how to handle them in a way that promotes trust and deepens your friendship. Find enrichment activities that provide mental and physical stimulation to make sure your box turtle has a happy and healthy life.

Explore the social dimensions of box turtle behavior, deciphering their signals of communication and gaining insight into their distinct personalities. We'll also examine many box turtle species in more detail, offering insightful information to assist you in selecting the ideal companion.

As we go, we'll cover grooming tips to ensure your box turtle's shell remains healthy and vibrant. Discover the many phases of their life cycle, from hatchling to adulthood, to develop a greater respect for these amazing animals.

Lastly, we'll cover commonly asked topics, dispelling falsehoods and providing useful answers to typical issues. Prepare to go on a fulfilling adventure of exploration and friendship with your box turtle as we go through the fundamentals of ethical ownership in this extensive handbook."

Chapter 1

Selecting the Ideal Environment: Building a Comfortable House for Your Box Turtle

Making sure your box turtle has the ideal habitat is essential to its general happiness and well-being. Because of their terrestrial lifestyle, box turtles need an environment that is meticulously designed to resemble their native habitat. We'll examine the essential components of creating an appropriate habitat in this in-depth analysis, taking into account variables like enclosure size, substrate, temperature, lighting, and enrichment.

Knowing the native Habitat: It's important to comprehend the box turtle's native habitat before delving into the details of an artificial one. These reptiles can be found in a range of habitats, including damp meadows, grasslands, and forests. They usually look for locations to burrow for security, as well as spots that provide access to both shade and sunlight. We will be able to replicate a habitat that supports our box turtle's well-being by bearing these factors in mind.

Size and Design of the Enclosure: Keeping your box turtle healthy depends heavily on the enclosure's size. Greater activity and more natural behaviors are possible in a larger enclosure. A habitat that is at least four feet by four feet is advised for a single adult box turtle. You should modify the enclosure size if you intend to keep more than one turtle.

Use materials like wood or durable plastic for the enclosure walls to create a safe and impenetrable habitat. Make sure you have enough ventilation to keep a healthy air exchange, which will stop humidity from building up and perhaps cause respiratory problems.

Selecting the Correct Substratum: Digging and burrowing are examples of natural behaviors that can be facilitated by selecting the proper substrate, which is necessary to replicate the natural environment. For the required texture and moisture retention, a blend of cypress mulch, coconut coir, and organic topsoil works well. For thermoregulation and nesting behaviors, your box turtle has to be able to dig, so the substrate needs to be deep enough for it to do so.

Temperature Gradient: The health of your box turtle depends on the enclosure's ability to maintain a suitable temperature gradient. Since these reptiles are ectothermic, their body temperature is controlled by outside heat sources. Assign a temperature range of 90 to 95 degrees Fahrenheit (32 to 35 degrees Celsius) for the basking area. The temperature on the colder side of the cage should be between 21 and 24 degrees Celsius, or 70 to 75 degrees Fahrenheit. To reach and maintain these temperature zones, use under-tank heating pads or heat-emitting bulbs.

UVB Lighting: In order to properly metabolize calcium and preserve the health of their shell and bones, box turtles need to be exposed to ultraviolet B (UVB) light. Box turtles absorb UVB rays by basking in sunshine in their natural habitat. It's critical to recreate this in captivity with UVB-emitting lamps. To ensure maximum efficiency, make sure the bulbs offer the proper UVB spectrum and replace them as the manufacturer recommends.

Hiding Spots and Enrichment: To help your box turtle feel less stressed and more secure, make sure the habitat has hiding places. Include hiding spots by including half logs, bushes, or other structures as shelters. Incorporate climbing and exploring items as well, since box turtles like to explore their environment.

Maintaining the mental and physical health of your box turtle requires enrichment. Introduce objects that will pique their curiosity and promote natural behaviors, such as branches, logs, and rocks. To maintain a lively and interesting atmosphere, think about frequently moving or rotating these pieces.

Water Source: It's essential for your box turtle's general health and hydration to have a clean, easily accessible water source. Offer a large sufficiently shallow water dish for sipping and soaking. Make sure the water is changed frequently to minimize contamination, and keep an eye on the humidity levels to keep the enclosure from becoming overly damp.

Routine care: To guarantee that your box turtle lives in a clean and healthy environment, routine habitat care is necessary. To stop the growth of bacteria and parasites, remove waste, uneaten food, and any filthy substrate on a regular basis. At least once a month, give the enclosure a thorough cleaning, replacing the substrate and sanitizing any surfaces that require it.

Tracking Health and Behavior: It's critical to keep an eye on your box turtle's behavior to identify any health problems early on. Observe eating patterns, basking activity, and any changes in appearance or signs of lethargy. Plan routine health check-ups with a reptile veterinarian, and seek professional assistance as soon as you discover any problems.

In conclusion, furnishing your box turtle with a comfortable and appropriate home is an enjoyable project that immediately enhances its quality of life. Your box turtle will thrive in captivity if you can comprehend and replicate its natural habitat, as well as provide appropriate temperature gradients, UVB lighting, hiding spots, and enrichment. To ensure that you have a happy and long-lasting relationship with these amazing reptiles, appropriate ownership involves regular monitoring, upkeep, and veterinarian care. Recall that the cornerstone of your box turtle's happy and healthy existence is a well-designed habitat.

Chapter 2

Feeding Frenzy: Box Turtles' Nutritional Needs and Dietary Advice

A nutritious and well-balanced diet is essential for your box turtle's long-term health. This in-depth examination of eating behaviors will cover the natural diet of box turtles, the dietary needs that are critical to their health, and useful dietary advice to maintain the health of your shelled friend.

Recognizing the Natural Diet: Being omnivores, box turtles in the natural eat a variety of plant and animal materials. Their natural diet could consist of a variety of flora, fruits, vegetables, worms, slugs, snails, and insects. It is imperative to replicate this diversity in captivity in order to supply the vital nutrients that box turtles require in order to remain in maximum health.

Equilibrium Dietary Components:

1. Protein: An essential part of a box turtle's diet, protein aids in the development of its muscles and shell. Good sources of protein include earthworms, mealworms, slugs, and crickets. To guarantee a diet that is well-rounded, provide a range of protein sources.

2. Vegetables: Rich in vitamins and minerals include dark, leafy greens like kale, collard greens, and dandelion greens. To provide a variety of nutrients, add carrots, bell peppers, and squash in addition to these. To make vegetables easier to eat, chop or shred them into bite-sized pieces.

3. Fruits: Because of their high sugar content, fruits ought to be served in moderation. As occasional treats, add berries, melons, and little portions of apple or pear. To avoid spoiling, take out any fruits that haven't been consumed yet.

4. Calcium: The growth of shells and the general health of bones depend on calcium. Give the food a calcium boost by scattering some calcium powder or a cuttlebone over it. Furthermore, UVB light exposure facilitates the absorption of calcium.

5. Commercial Diets: One easy approach to make sure box turtles get a balanced nutritional profile is to use premium commercial turtle pellets or diets designed especially for them. They should, however, be supplemented with fresh foods and not be the only thing in their diet.

Feeding Frequency: Your box turtle's age and activity level determine how frequently it should be fed. While juvenile box turtles may need daily feeding to encourage their growth, adult box turtles can be fed every two to three days. You can make sure your turtles get enough nutrients without going overboard by keeping an eye on their behavior and modifying the feeding plan accordingly.

Hydration: A shallow dish of fresh, clean water is vital for box turtles to be properly hydrated. Giving box turtles access to a larger container is advantageous because some of them might prefer to soak in water. To avoid infection, make sure the water is changed on a regular basis.

Dietary Advice: 1. Variety Is Essential
In addition to ensuring that the box turtles get a wide variety of nutrients, providing a varied assortment of foods helps mimic the natural diet of the species. To keep their food varied and nourishing, try out new fruits, veggies, and protein sources.

2. Gut Loading Insects: If you feed insects, think about giving them foods high in nutrients right before you give

them to your box turtle. This improves the insects' nutritional content, which in turn improves the turtle's diet.

3. Check the Calcium-to-Phosphorus Ratio: It's important to keep the calcium-to-phosphorus ratio at the right level. Feeding high-phosphorus foods (e.g., some insects or meats) in excess can result in metabolic bone disease and a calcium deficit.

4. Seasonal Variations: Depending on the season, box turtles may exhibit variations in appetite. Their metabolism slows down in the cooler months, so they might consume less. To guarantee they stay in good health, change the frequency of their feedings and keep an eye on their weight.

5. Pay Attention to Chewing Habits: The beaks of box turtles are made for tearing, not grinding. Reduce the

size of the vegetable pieces you chop or shred to make eating and digesting simpler.

6. Steer Clear of poisonous Foods: Onions, garlic, and high-oxalate greens like spinach are among the foods that can be poisonous to box turtles. Learn which foods are harmful and safe to eat in order to avoid accidental injury.

Dietary Guidelines for Different Life Stages:

1. Hatchlings: Compared to adults, hatchlings have distinct dietary needs, with a focus on protein for growth. To accommodate their smaller stature and growing jaws, serve them finely chopped veggies and small, soft invertebrates.

2. Adults: Box turtles should eat a more well-balanced diet of veggies and protein as they get older. Adapt the food schedule to their reduced metabolic rate.

In summary:

To ensure that your box turtle receives the nourishment they require, carefully balance protein, fruits, veggies, and supplements. You can make sure your box turtle has a balanced and healthy diet by learning about their natural diet, offering a variety of foods, and taking age-specific needs into account. Responsible turtle ownership includes regular behavior and weight monitoring as well as modifying food schedules as necessary. You may extend the life and health of your box turtle friend by paying close attention to details and making a commitment to their nutrition.

Chapter 3

Box Turtle Health: Typical Problems and Proactive Treatment

Keeping your box turtle healthy is an essential part of being a good owner. We will go into frequent health problems that box turtles face, how to take care of them in advance to keep them healthy, and how crucial it is to take them to the vet on a regular basis.

Recognizing Common Health Concerns:

1. infected respiratory systems:

Respiratory infections in box turtles can occur, frequently as a result of insufficient temperature or humidity levels. Lethargy, wheezing, and nasal discharge are possible symptoms. Respiratory problems can be avoided by making sure the enclosure has a well-controlled temperature gradient and enough ventilation.

2. Rotting Shells:

A fungal or bacterial infection that damages the shell, shell rot is frequently brought on by extended exposure to moist or unclean environments. It appears on the shell as soft areas, discolouration, or an off-putting smell. Shell rot must be prevented and treated with care, requiring regular shell examinations and the maintenance of a clean, dry habitat.

3. MBD, or metabolic bone disease:

A calcium deficit causes metabolic bone disease, which weakens bones and causes shell abnormalities. It may happen if there is an imbalance in the diet's calcium-to-phosphorus ratio or if there is insufficient UVB exposure. Important preventive steps include giving a calcium supplement, providing UVB lighting, and making sure a diet is balanced.

4. Parasitic Diseases:

Box turtles may experience symptoms from internal or external parasites, including changes in appetite, lethargy, and diarrhea. A veterinarian's routine fecal examinations can aid in the diagnosis and management of parasite illnesses. Preventing parasite problems also involves feeding them a healthy food and keeping the enclosure clean.

5. Females' Binding of Eggs:

When laying their eggs, female box turtles may encounter difficulties with a process called "egg-binding." This happens when they don't have enough calcium in their diets or nesting places, for example, which prevents them from laying eggs. Egg-binding can be avoided by offering a good nesting space with the right substrate and making sure the food is high in calcium.

6. Dehydration:

Box turtles are frequently concerned about dehydration, which can be brought on by insufficient water intake or a very dry habitat. Important preventive steps include keeping an eye on your turtle's hydration levels and providing a shallow water dish. Another way to keep your turtle hydrated is to sometimes submerge it in water.

Preventive Care Interventions:

1. Appropriate Design of Habitat:

The cornerstone of preventative care is the creation and upkeep of an optimal habitat. Make sure the enclosure has a clean substrate, the proper humidity levels, and a temperature gradient. Keep the enclosure clean on a regular basis to avoid the growth of parasites and bacteria.

2. Sufficient Lighting

A box turtle's general health depends on its exposure to UVB radiation because it promotes healthy calcium metabolism. Purchase premium UVB bulbs and make sure to change them in accordance with the manufacturer's instructions. When feasible, let your turtle enjoy some natural sunlight, but be mindful of the possibility of overheating.

3. A well-rounded diet

Preventing nutritional deficits requires eating a diet that is well-balanced. Give your box turtle a diverse range of fruits, veggies, and proteins to make sure it gets all the nutrition it needs. Add extra calcium to their diet to maintain healthy bones and shells.

4. Frequent Medical Examinations:

Make time for routine check-ups with a veterinarian who specializes in reptile care. Fecal examinations, health assessments, and any concerns you may have can all be handled by a licensed veterinarian. Effective treatment of health disorders depends on early detection.

5. Handling Hydration:

Preventing dehydration requires maintaining proper hydrated. Make sure your box turtle always has access to fresh, clean water. In order to help your turtle stay hydrated, you might want to immerse them in shallow water if they show symptoms of dehydration, such as sunken eyes or lethargy.

6. Using observational monitoring

Keep a close eye on the behavior, eating, and general look of your box turtle. Behavior changes, weight loss, or anomalies in the shell could be signs of underlying medical problems. As soon as you have any concerns, speak with a veterinarian.

7. New Items in Quarantine:

Consider putting your collection under quarantine if you're adding a new box turtle. This aids in keeping potential illnesses or parasites from infecting already-existing turtle populations. Keep a tight eye out for any signs of disease in the new arrival during the quarantine period.

8. Safe Work Procedures:

Take good care of your box turtle to reduce stress and potential harm. To avoid putting undue strain on the turtle's limbs or shell, handle it sparingly and support its entire body when needed. Stress can weaken the immune system, increasing the turtle's vulnerability to illnesses.

Emergency Reaction:

Even with precautions taken, emergencies can still happen. It's critical to know how to react in case of a health emergency:

1. Breathing Problems:

If the turtle exhibits symptoms of respiratory distress, such as difficulty breathing, place it in a warm environment and keep it segregated. See a veterinarian right away because respiratory problems might worsen quickly.

2. Shell Damage:

If the turtle has damage to its shell, do not try to heal it yourself. To evaluate the extent of the injury and choose the best course of action, get emergency veterinarian care.

3. Lethargic and Appetite Deficit:

Lethargy or an appetite deficit in your box turtle may be signs of an underlying health problem. Set the turtle aside, keep a watchful eye on its behavior, and seek advice from a veterinarian.

In summary:

Your box turtle need early veterinary treatment, frequent monitoring, and preventive actions to maintain good health. You can help ensure your box turtle companion lives a long and healthy life by being aware of common health issues, designing their habitat appropriately, feeding them a balanced diet, and responding to any concerns right away. Recall that the secret to making sure your box turtle has a happy, healthy, and meaningful existence in captivity is to provide proactive care.

Chapter 4

Handling with Care: Building Trust and Bonding with Your Box Turtle

A satisfying part of owning a reptile is developing a close relationship and earning your box turtle's confidence. Box turtles tend to be solitary and somewhat shy, in contrast to species that are more gregarious. It takes time, tolerance, understanding, and respect for their innate tendencies to build trust. We'll go into the nuances of caring for box turtles, the value of earning their trust, and useful advice to help you and your shelled friend have a fulfilling and positive relationship in this in-depth investigation.

Recognizing the Character of Box Turtles:
Because they are more shy by nature, box turtles might become stressed out if they are handled frequently.

They are not gregarious creatures like dogs or cats and generally prefer isolation. It's important to acknowledge that not all box turtles will welcome handling and to respect their need for privacy.

1. The Key Is Patience:
It takes time to establish confidence with a box turtle. When building a relationship, patience is an essential quality. Don't try to handle your turtle right away; instead, let it get used to its new surroundings. Take time to watch how they behave, take note of their comfort zones, and honor their need for privacy.

2. Slow Introductory:
When introducing handling, start gradually. Start with brief sessions and let the turtle investigate its surroundings and your hand at its own speed. Steer clear of abrupt movements or hurried attempts to pick up the turtle right away since this might be stressful.

Gradual exposure increases comfort level and lessens the possibility that handling will be associated negatively.

3. Hand Acquaintance:

Give your box turtle some time to become used to you before trying to handle them. Spend some time in close proximity to their enclosure, speaking softly and moving gently. This facilitates the turtle's association of your presence with a safe haven.

4. The Appropriate Moment:

Select the appropriate moment to handle. During the warmer hours of the day, box turtles are most active. Refrain from awakening them in the middle of the night or early morning when this is when they naturally go to sleep. Positive interactions are more likely to occur when handling occurs when they are inherently more awake and active.

5. Identifying Stress Indicators:

It's critical to comprehend stress signs. Box turtles may exhibit symptoms of stress like as retreating into their shell, breathing quickly, hissing, or exhibiting a pronounced withdrawal reaction. Return the turtle to its enclosure right away and let it hide if you notice any indications of stress.

6. Technique for Supportive Handling:

When you believe your box turtle is ready to be handled, approach it from the side, slowly and carefully. Using both hands, raise the turtle so that its torso is supported and its legs are not overly compressed. Because box turtles are not nimble and can sustain injuries from even small accidents, make sure you have a firm grasp to avoid unintentional slips.

7. Brief but Encouraging Sessions:

Initially, keep handling sessions brief. As your turtle grows more comfortable being held, gradually extend the time. Always end the sessions on a positive note, returning the turtle to its enclosure respectfully. Over time, developing positive connections with handling helps to establish trust.

8. The Importance of Body Language:

Box turtles use body language to convey messages. During handling, pay heed to their cues. It's important to respect their boundaries and let them go back to their enclosure if they withdraw into their shell or show signs of distress.

9. Establish a Secure Handling Setting:

Select a safe and peaceful area for handling. Steer clear of loud noises, abrupt movements, and other possible stressors for your box turtle. A serene and regulated setting fosters a favorable encounter for both you and your turtle.

10. Sweets and Encouraging Behavior:

Treats help to create a positive association between handling and handling. Small, turtle-friendly goodies can be provided during and after handling to develop pleasant connections. To avoid overfeeding, moderation is essential.

11. Regularity in Communication:

To develop trust, you must be consistent in your interactions. Gradually building trust involves regular, gentle handling sessions along with monitoring the turtle's comfort level. Box turtles value routines that are maintained with consistency.

12. Include Enrichment

During handling sessions, include enrichment activities to keep your box turtle's mind active. This may entail putting them in a safe, supervised outdoor enclosure or providing safe objects for exploration. Positive associations with handling and mental stimulation are enhanced by enrichment.

13. Honor each person's unique personality:
Every box turtle has a distinct character. While some might always prefer minimal interaction, others might grow more accepting of handling. Honor their personal choices and acknowledge that a close relationship can take many forms.

14. Examine Typical Behaviors:
When touching your box turtle, let it exhibit its normal behaviors. This could be taking a nap in your hands, climbing, or simply exploring. Comprehending and

adapting to these actions improves the relationship as a whole.

15. Keep an Eye Out for Enjoyment Signs:
Look for indications that the interaction is enjoyable for your box turtle. These could be as simple as adopting a comfortable stance, exploring slowly, or even stretching their limbs. Positive indicators show that handling your turtle is starting to feel more natural.

16. Exploration in the outdoors:
For your box turtle, supervised outside exploration can be a rewarding experience. Construct a safe outside enclosure that receives plenty of sunshine. Spending time outside offers more stimulation and a change of scenery.

17. Frequent Health Examinations:

Take advantage of handling sessions to perform mild health checks. Inspect the mouth, nose, and eyes for discharge indications. Examine the shell for damage or irregularities. Frequent health examinations aid in the early identification of possible problems.

18. Using When Receiving Veterinary Care:
When receiving veterinary care, frequent handling could be required. You must gradually adapt your box turtle to handling, particularly if it needs medical care. In order to prepare them for veterinary visits, gentle and consistent handling in non-stressful situations is helpful.

In summary:
With your box turtle, developing trust and a close friendship is a gradual but worthwhile process. Observation, patience, and tactful management are the essentials for building a strong rapport. Keep in mind that every box turtle is different and that not all of them

will accept handling. You can build a solid relationship that improves the health and enrichment of your box turtle partner by getting to know them, staying within their boundaries, and making good associations. Mutual trust must be developed, and as you give your box turtle the time and attention it deserves, you'll discover that your relationship with it grows stronger and becomes a satisfying and enduring one.

Chapter 5

Enrichment Activities: Maintaining the Happiness and Stimulation of Your Box Turtle

Your box turtle's general happiness and well-being depend heavily on enrichment activities. These reptiles gain a great deal from mental and physical stimulation even though they are often solitary and may not display social behaviors. We'll cover the value of enrichment for box turtles, different kinds of enrichment activities, and how to set up an interesting habitat that will keep your box turtle happy and stimulated in this in-depth investigation.

Recognizing the Value of Enrichment
Creating an atmosphere that stimulates natural behaviors, mental activity, and physical activity is the

goal of enrichment. A well-enriched habitat benefits box turtles in the following ways:

1. Psychological Excitation:
Box turtles find engaging activities stimulating, which keeps them from getting bored and improves their mental health.

2. Exercise Physically:
Engaging in enrichment activities promotes exploration and mobility, which in turn encourages physical exercise—a vital component of good health.

3. Expression of Behavior:
Box turtles live longer when their normal habits are allowed to occur. This covers digging, climbing, and exploring, among other things.

4. Reducing Stress:

By giving natural behaviors a place to be expressed and avoiding the detrimental consequences of boredom, a stimulating environment lowers stress.

Different Enrichment Activity Types:

1. Activities for Foraging:

Provide opportunities for natural foraging by hiding food in various locations throughout the enclosure. The turtles become more active as they explore and look for their food since this also enhances their sense of smell.

2. Exploring Prospects:

Diggers by nature, box turtles are. Give them a substrate that enables them to perform digging activities. They can burrow and bury themselves in places mixed with soil, coconut coir, or cypress mulch, which simulates their original environment.

3. Climbing Frameworks:

Box turtles enjoy having low structures to climb upon, even though they are not enthusiastic climbers. Their enclosure can be enhanced with pebbles, logs, or even modest platforms to allow them to explore different levels and participate in light climbing exercises.

4. Water-related Features:

Give your box turtle access to a shallow water dish or even a tiny water area so it may soak. This gives them access to water and let them to engage in natural activities like soaking and wading, which are crucial for the preservation of their skin and shells.

5. Natural Components:

Include organic components in the enclosure, such as branches, leaves, and non-toxic plants. These components create visual obstacles, hiding places, and a more organic, dynamic setting.

6. New Items:

Periodically add fresh items to the enclosure. Safe products like non-toxic toys, mirrors that are safe for reptiles, or even balls that are big enough for the turtle to move around can be included in this category. The unveiling of new things sparks interest and inquiry.

7. Exploration in the outdoors:

Enrichment through supervised outside time in a safe, secure environment is highly recommended. Their overall well-being is greatly enhanced by exposure to daylight, various textures, and outside elements.

8. Engaging in Conspecific Interaction:

If you have more than one box turtle, enrichment can be achieved through controlled contact. This should be done carefully, though, and people should be kept an eye out for any aggressive behavior.

9. Intense Perception:

Change the environment to stimulate their senses. Periodically, new noises, smells, and textures can be added. This can be setting out safe objects with different textures or providing a variety of food options for them to try.

10. Enrichment item rotation:

Make frequent rotations and changes to the enrichment materials to avoid habituation. This maintains the environment's energy and keeps the turtle from growing bored with its surroundings.

Establishing a Rich Environment

1. Ideal Enclosure Architecture:

Create the enclosure with the box turtles' natural behaviors in mind. A water source, a basking area with a temperature gradient, and hiding places should all be present. To make digging easier, use natural substrates such as soil, coir from coconuts, or mulch made from cypress.

2. Non-toxic and safe materials:

Make sure new things are manufactured from non-toxic and safe materials when introducing them. Steer clear of anything with little pieces that could be consumed. In order to create an environment that is enriching, safety comes first.

3. Different Diet:

Adjust their diet such that it reflects the variety of foods they would find in the wild. This helps them meet their dietary needs and gives mealtimes something new to look forward to.

4. Remark and Modification:

Analyze your box turtle's behavior on a regular basis to determine how well enrichment activities are working. If there are things or activities that kids seem particularly interested in, think about bringing those elements of their environment closer to them.

5. Outside Cabinets:

Provide people the chance to explore the outdoors if at all possible. Build a safe, open-air shelter that receives plenty of natural light. Box turtles can encounter a variety of weather conditions and participate in more strenuous physical activity when they are outside.

6. Regularity in Routine:

Continue the daily schedule in a consistent manner while adding enriching activities. This increases the box turtles' sense of security and trust in their surroundings.

7. With Attention to Detail:

Make sure handling is a fulfilling and enjoyable experience. Their mental and physical health is enhanced by handling sessions that involve gentle interactions and letting them explore.

Extra Suggestions for Activities That Enrich:

1. Teaching Aids:

Think of including instructional toys made for reptiles. During eating, they can use puzzle feeders or treat-dispensing devices to stimulate their cognitive abilities.

2. Communication via Glass:

You can encourage interaction with very bashful box turtles by pressing an object or your palm up against the glass. This frees them from handling so they can watch and investigate.

3. Outdoor Environment Rotation:

If you offer an outside enclosure, think about moving it around from time to time. This provides a continuously evolving and fascinating outdoor experience by introducing fresh smells, sounds, and views.

4. Seasonal Variations

Adapt enrichment activities to the changing seasons. For instance, you can increase the amount of outside activities during the warmer months and concentrate on inside enrichment during the colder ones.

5. Consulting with Specialists:

For more suggestions catered to the requirements of your particular box turtle, consult with veterinarians, reptile behaviorists, or specialists in reptiles. They can shed light on the habits and inclinations unique to a species.

In summary:

Enrichment activities are a crucial part of caring for box turtles in an ethical manner, as they greatly enhance their general pleasure and well-being. It is possible to establish a setting that promotes physical health, mental stimulation, and the natural expression of behaviors in box turtles by learning about their natural habits and introducing a variety of engaging activities into their daily existence. Keep in mind that every box turtle is unique and has different tastes. Observe their responses, modify your activities accordingly, and have the satisfying feeling of giving your box turtle friend a full and happy existence.

Chapter 6

Social Creatures: An Understanding of Communication and Behavior in Box Turtles

To give the best care and promote a peaceful connection with these fascinating reptiles, it is essential to comprehend the behavior and communication patterns of box turtles. Though they lack the innate social nature of certain animals, box turtles display distinct behaviors and modes of communication that mirror their inclinations, requirements, and reactions to their surroundings. We'll delve into the subtleties of box turtle behavior, communication indicators, and the significance of understanding their actions to guarantee a happy and healthy existence in this in-depth investigation.

Recognizing the Behavior of Box Turtles:

1. Behavior in Territories:

Territoriality is a well-known characteristic of box turtles. In the wild, they create home ranges and defend their regions. They might act territorially when kept in captivity, particularly if kept with other box turtles. To reduce territorial disputes, enough space and resources must be provided.

2. The propensity toward hibernation:

Box turtles naturally hibernate during the winter. As the temperature drops and the number of daylight hours decreases, they may exhibit behavioral changes, such as increased burrowing tendencies and decreased activity. An proper hibernation habitat must be supplied for their welfare.

3. Heat regulation as well as basking:

For survival, box turtles require sun exposure. They need access to a basking area with an appropriate temperature gradient in order to regulate their body temperature. Digestion, metabolism, and vitamin D generation are all aided by this activity.

4. Digging & Burrowing:

Due to their innate digging instincts, box turtles may dig in captivity in order to explore, locate hiding places, or build nests. Their innate tendencies are supported when a substrate, such soil or coconut coir, is provided that permits digging.

5. Investigating and Gathering:

Curious animals, box turtles like to investigate their surroundings. They forage, locating food with the help of their acute sense of smell. Promoting inquiry through a range of environmental cues benefits their mental health.

6. Seeking Refuge:

When the weather becomes bad or they sense danger, box turtles look for cover. Giving them hiding places, shelters, or half-log buildings lets them feel safe and comfortable while they're in captivity.

7. Soaking and Sunbathing:

For box turtles, sunbathing and soaking are key activities. Their physical health is enhanced by exposure to natural sunlight, which encourages the production of vitamin D. By providing a shallow water dish, you let them to participate in soaking behaviors, which promote shell health and hydration.

Cues for Communication:

Box turtles express themselves through a variety of indications and actions, even though they might not communicate in the same manner as social animals. Recognizing these signs of communication is essential to determining their requirements and creating a stress-free and happy atmosphere.

1. Disclosing and Withdrawing:

A box turtle's retreat or hiding behind its shell can indicate a need for seclusion or a reaction to danger. It is vital to their welfare to honor their demand for privacy at these times.

2. Slow Motion:

In general, box turtles move slowly and deliberately. Frantic or fast movements might be a sign of anxiety, discomfort, or a reaction to something being seen as a threat. Their general well-being can be assessed by observing their movement patterns.

3. Movement of the Head and Limbs:

Box turtles use their delicate movements to communicate. A person may nod or bob their head in reaction to an outside stimulus or as a show of acknowledgment. Leg gestures like extending or withdrawing the legs can convey comfort or pain.

4. Voices:

Although they don't vocalize as much as some other reptiles, box turtles can make hissing noises when they feel frightened or uneasy. Since this may be a defensive action, it's important to talk to them gently in order to prevent tension.

5. Feeding and Cues for Appetite:

Their eating habits reveal information about their general well-being and contentment. A box turtle that is healthy and receiving enough food will show interest in eating, but an abrupt loss of appetite could indicate underlying problems that need to be addressed.

6. Preferences for Basking:

Box turtles use their basking habit to express their preferred temperature. Frequent basking suggests that they are controlling their body temperature, however avoidance of the basking area could be an indication of discomfort or discontentment with the temperature difference.

7. The Soaking Behavior

Soaking behavior is a way to express the need for water. Providing them with a shallow water dish enables them to control their level of hydration, and monitoring their soaking behaviors guarantees that they have access to enough water.

8. Angry and Protective Positions:

Defensive postures may result from territorial disputes or perceived threats. Aggression in box turtles can manifest as head raises, limb extensions, or hissing noises. Taking action against environmental stressors or separating individuals can help reduce aggressive behavior.

Environmental Aspects Influencing Conduct:

1. Lighting and Temperature:

Box turtle behavior is greatly influenced by the enclosure's temperature and lighting. Stress and health problems might result from insufficient UVB exposure or inadequate basking temperatures. Sufficient lighting and heating systems are essential for their welfare.

2. Layout and Size of Enclosures:

Box turtle behavior is influenced by the enclosure's dimensions and design. Stress and territorial conflicts can result from inadequate space, but natural behaviors are supported in a well-designed environment that has hiding places, basking areas, and suitable substrates.

3. Social Structure:

Behavior in multi-turtle ecosystems is influenced by social dynamics. Stress can be brought on by territorial disputes, dominance tendencies, or imbalances in gender roles. A peaceful living environment depends on your understanding of the social dynamics of your box turtles and on giving them lots of room.

4. Conspecific Presence:

Behavior can be affected by the presence of other box turtles. Box turtles are solitary creatures in general, although they can also engage in social interactions or display territorial characteristics. By keeping an eye on their interactions and offering sufficient resources, possible stress is reduced.

5. Seasonal Variations

In response to variations in the weather, box turtles may display characteristics like decreased activity in the winter or increased foraging in the summer. Their biological cycles can be supported by imitating the seasonal fluctuations found in their natural surroundings.

Creating a Connection via Observation:

1. Regular Communication:

Building trust requires polite but consistent interaction. Spend some time in close proximity to the enclosure, use calming language, and watch how they behave. If they feel comfortable doing so, gradual handling exposure promotes a healthy bond.

2. Hand Feeding:

Giving food by hand can foster favorable associations. Give them their favorite snacks so they will come to link your presence with good things. This reduces handling-related stress and fosters trust.

3. Observation in Routine:

Make it a routine to watch the activity of your box turtle. Check for indicators of stress, changes in appetite, and changes in activity level on a regular basis. Early behavioral change identification enables timely intervention.

4. courtesy about one's personal space
It's important to honor their demand for private space. Even if they need to connect, their comfort is guaranteed when they can withdraw to hiding places or have solitude when engaging in particular behaviors.

5. Encouragement that is constructive:
Desired behaviors can be reinforced by providing snacks or other forms of positive reinforcement. Rewarding them for favorable behaviors or demonstrating interest in an enrichment item encourages them to repeat those actions.

Common Issues with Behavior:

1. Stress-Related Actions:

Stress can show up as a variety of symptoms, such as changes in appetite, fatigue, or defensive body language. For their wellbeing, it is essential to recognize and deal with stresses such improper enclosure conditions or environmental changes.

2. Hostility Among Multiple Turtles:

Aggression or territorial disputes can arise in areas where there are several box turtles. Creating a lot of space, keeping an eye on social dynamics, and dividing people apart if needed can all assist control hostility.

3. Passivity or Absence of Inquiry:

Reduced exploration or a lack of activity could be indicators of environmental unhappiness or health problems. It is imperative to guarantee ideal habitat conditions, offer diverse enrichment, and attend to any possible health issues.

4. Refusing to Consume:

When someone suddenly refuses to eat, they need help. It could be a sign of stress, medical conditions, or food allergies. It is important to consult a veterinarian to rule out underlying health conditions and to make dietary or environmental adjustments.

In summary:

It takes patience, careful observation, and a profound appreciation of the peculiarities of box turtles to fully comprehend the behavior and communication of these dynamic creatures. You may develop a pleasant and fulfilling relationship with these amazing reptiles by reading their signs, honoring their innate instincts, and providing a setting that promotes their well-being. A flourishing and happy box turtle partner is the result of attentive care, regular observation, and habitat modifications. You'll discover that every encounter you have with them offers insightful information about the amazing world of box turtles as you set out on this adventure to comprehend their behavior.

Chapter 7

Species Spotlight: Examining Various Box Turtle Varieties for Pets

As members of the genus Terrapene, box turtles are interesting reptiles distinguished by their various kinds and distinctive features. Box turtles are popular pets because of their unique behaviors, hues, and shell patterns. We'll examine many box turtle species that are frequently kept as pets in this thorough analysis, stressing each species' unique traits, maintenance needs, and things prospective owners should know.

Turtle: Terrapene carolina carolina, Eastern Box Turtle
Physical attributes:
The distinctive domed carapace of the Eastern Box Turtle is decorated with elaborate patterns that range in color from orange to brown. The turtle's high, movable

shell enables it to entirely enclose itself for protection. They frequently exhibit bright colors, such as orange, yellow, or red, on their head and legs.

Range and Habitat:

Eastern Box Turtles are found in the eastern United States and live in grasslands, meadows, and deciduous woodlands, among other habitats. They do best in places with lots of vegetation and access to both land and shallow water.

Taking Care of Things:

Set up the enclosure: Make sure it's roomy and filled with a mixture of dirt, moss, and leaf litter. Add several hiding places and a shallow dish for soaking in water.

Eastern Box Turtles eat a variety of foods. Provide a well-rounded diet that includes fruits, leafy greens, worms, and insects.

- Temperature and Lighting: For optimal shell and bone health, maintain a temperature gradient and use UVB lighting.

- Interaction: Eastern Box Turtles can display recognition and curiosity towards their owners, even though they might not be as gregarious as some other reptiles. Honor their demand for privacy and don't interfere too much to prevent tension.

Terrapene carolina triunguis, the three-toed box turtle:

Physical attributes:

The Eastern Box Turtle and the Three-Toed Box Turtle are similar in that both are distinguished by having three toes on each of their hind feet. Its carapace comes in a range of colors, including as olive, black, and brown. One important marker is the quantity of toe scales.

Range and Habitat:

The range of the Three-Toed Box Turtle stretches into portions of Mexico and the central United States. It is more common in open woodlands and grasslands, where the soil is loose and sandy.

Taking Care of Things:

- Establish a densely planted enclosure on a sandy substrate. Add places to hide and a shallow water dish for washing and drinking.
- Diet: All food is consumed by Three-Toed Box Turtles. Serve a variety of foods, such as fruits, vegetables, snails, and insects.
- Temperature and Lighting: Make UVB lighting available as well as a temperature gradient. The metabolism of calcium and thermoregulation depend on these components.
- Interaction: Three-Toed Box Turtles are similar to Eastern Box Turtles in that they may show signs of

recognition but prefer little or no interaction. Make sure everything is calm to prevent tension.

Terrapene ornata, the Ornate Box Turtle:

Physical attributes:

The highly unusual Ornate Box Turtle is distinguished by its high, domed shell, which is dotted with radiating golden lines. Its shell comes in a variety of colors, including as orange, black, and brown. Generally speaking, guys exhibit more vibrant hues than females.

Range and Habitat:

Ornate Box Turtles are native to the central United States, where they live in open forests, grasslands, and prairies. They do well in environments with sand-filled, loose soil.

Taking Care of Things:

- Setup for Enclosure: Use a substrate of sandy soil or a sand-soil mixture to replicate their native environment. As well as a shallow water dish for drinking and soaking, provide hiding places.

- Food: Although they are omnivores, Ornate Box Turtles have a fondness for a range of plant materials, insects, and snails.

- Temperature and Lighting: For optimum health, maintain appropriate temperatures and provide UVB lighting. Having a place to bask is essential for thermoregulation.

- Contact: Although Ornate Box Turtles could be more tolerant of handling than certain other species, restrict your interactions with them to prevent stress. Give them lots of places to hide so they may feel safe.

Turtles of the Gulf Coast (Terrapene carolina major):

Physical attributes:

A high-domed carapace and varying coloring define the Gulf Coast Box Turtle, a subspecies of the Eastern Box Turtle. Their head, legs, and shells can all have colorful patterns and designs.

Range and Habitat:

Gulf Coast Box Turtles live in areas along the US Gulf Coast, as their name implies. They favor regions that are both open and wooded and have access to water.

Taking Care of Things:

- Establish an enclosure by combining dirt, leaf litter, and hiding places to create a habitat. Add a small dish of water for hydration and soaking.
- Food: As omnivores, Gulf Coast Box Turtles eat a variety of fruits, vegetables, worms, and insects.

- Temperature and Lighting: Make UVB lighting available as well as a temperature gradient. Areas that get sun are essential for thermoregulation.

- Interaction: It's important to keep an eye on the stress levels of Gulf Coast Box Turtles, even if they might tolerate occasional handling. Give them plenty of time to explore and be alone.

Terrapene ornata luteola, the Western Box Turtle:

Physical attributes:

A subspecies of the Ornate Box Turtle, the Western Box Turtle is distinguished by its unique shell design, which consists of radiating lines. Their colors range from orange and yellow to black and brown. Typically, men are more colorful than females.

- Range and Habitat:

- Western Box Turtles are found in grasslands, forests, and desert regions in the western United States. They do best on soil that is well-drained or sandy.

Taking Care of Things:

- Setup for Enclosure: Use a substrate of sandy soil or a sand-soil mixture to replicate their native environment. As well as a shallow water dish for drinking and soaking, provide hiding places.

- Food: Although they are omnivores, Western Box Turtles enjoy a range of plant materials, insects, and snails.

- Temperature and Lighting: For optimum health, maintain appropriate temperatures and provide UVB lighting. Areas that get sun are essential for thermoregulation.

- Interaction: Western Box Turtles enjoy minimal interaction but may tolerate handling, just like other box turtles. To relieve tension, create a calm space with hiding places.

Things to Think About for Possible Owners:

1. Legal Aspects to Take into Account:

Examine and comprehend national and international legislation pertaining to the ownership of box turtles before purchasing one. Permits may be needed for some species since they may be protected.

2. Duration of Life:

Some box turtles can live for several decades, which is a long lifespan. Potential owners need to be ready for a long-term commitment and the related duties.

3. Space Needs:

For them to explore, box turtles need enough room. Make sure the enclosure accommodates their natural habits by being roomy, lush with vegetation, and equipped with hiding places.

4. Nutritional Requirements:

It is essential to comprehend the food requirements of particular box turtle species. For their health, they need a well-balanced diet rich in fruits, vegetables, insects, and calcium supplements.

5. Veterinary Medical Attention:

Preventive care and early identification of potential health issues are made possible by routine veterinarian examinations. Locate a veterinarian with expertise caring for reptiles.

6. Enhancement of the Environment:

Add elements for exploration, hiding places, and sunbathing sections to make the enclosure more enjoyable. Keep them mentally engaged by rotating and adding new enrichment materials on a regular basis.

7. Control of Temperature:

Ensure that the enclosure's temperature gradients are appropriate. Box turtles' digestion, metabolism, and general health depend on outside heat sources.

8. Observance of Natural Behaviors

Box turtles have natural characteristics that should be respected, such as their desire for seclusion and little handling. Establish a space where they can follow their inclinations.

In summary:

Owning a box turtle may be an enthralling and fulfilling experience for reptile aficionados. Every species offers a variety of choices for potential owners by bringing its distinct traits, hues, and behaviors to the table. To ensure the longevity and well-being of box turtle variations, it is imperative to comprehend their unique requirements. Each species adds something unique to the diverse range of box turtles, whether it's the vivid colors of the Ornate Box Turtle, the unusual toe count of the Three-Toed Box Turtle, or the exquisite patterns of the Eastern Box Turtle. Taking good care of them, giving them a stimulating habitat, and appreciating their uniqueness as responsible pet owners all contribute to a happy and rewarding relationship with these amazing reptiles.

Chapter 8

Grooming Guidelines: Maintaining a Clean and Healthy Shell for Your Box Turtle

A box turtle's shell is an essential part of their body, both as a shield and an indicator of their general well-being. Taking good care of their shells is crucial to keeping these amazing reptiles healthy. This thorough tutorial will go over grooming tips that are aimed at giving your box turtle friend a clean, strong, and healthy shell.

Comprehending the Turtle Shell Box:

1. How Important the Shell Is

One characteristic that sets box turtles apart is their shell, which shields them from predators and the elements. The carapace, or top shell, and the plastron, or bottom shell, make up its two main components. The condition of the shell, which is composed of bone and covered with keratin, is a good indicator of the turtle's general health.

2. Growth and Development of Shell:
The shell of a box turtle varies significantly as it grows. The shell of a young turtle is more pliable and softer, but it gradually gets harder as it ages. A healthy shell develops as a result of environmental factors, UVB exposure, and proper diet.

3. Shell Problems and Anomalies:
The shells of box turtles can develop cracks, malformations, pyramiding, or shell rot. Raised shell scutes, or pyramiding, are a common complication of poor nutrition and dehydration. Fungal or bacterial infections, such as shell rot, can arise from unsanitary circumstances or environmental factors.

Tips for Maintaining a Healthy Shell:

1. Shell Health's Nutrition:

Eating a good diet is essential to keeping a healthy shell. Make sure the food your box turtle eats is balanced and contains a range of insects, worms, leafy greens, and foods high in calcium. The growth and strength of the shell depend on calcium.

2. Drinking plenty of water

Drinking enough water is essential for healthy shells. In the enclosure, provide a dish with shallow water for drinking and soaking. Through their epidermis, box turtles absorb water, maintaining the integrity of their shell and staying hydrated overall.

3. Sunshine and UVB Radiation:

Vitamin D synthesis requires exposure to UVB light or natural sunlight. This is important because vitamin D is needed for the absorption of calcium. Make sure your turtle spends a certain amount of time each day in the sun or under UVB light.

4. Keeping the Enclosure Clean:
Maintaining a clean environment is essential to avoiding shell problems. Clean the enclosure on a regular basis to get rid of any substrate that might hold moisture, trash, and uneaten food. Substrates that are unclean or wet might harbor bacteria or fungi.

5. Frequent Health Examinations:
Visually inspect the shell of your box turtle on a regular basis. Examine the area for any anomalies, discolorations, fractures, or modifications in its acute state. Prompt intervention is made possible by early issue detection.

6. Taking Care:

Treat your box turtle with kindness and consideration. Keep the shell from being overly stressed or compressed since this could cause injury. To avoid harm, support the plastron and carapace of your turtle when you lift it.

7. Avoiding Pyramiding

Pyramiding is a frequent problem in box turtles kept in captivity and is frequently linked to poor nutrition and dehydration. To stop pyramiding, give a balanced meal, refrain from overfeeding, and make sure everyone has access to clean water.

8. Handling Deformities of the Shell:See a reptile veterinarian right once if you discover any abnormalities in the shell of your box turtle. Deformities may be a sign of incorrect environmental conditions, metabolic problems, or nutritional inadequacies.

9. How to Treat Shell Rot:

Shell rot needs to be treated right away. See a veterinarian if you see any symptoms, such as soft areas, discolouration, or bad odor. Topical antifungal or antibacterial drugs, as well as better living circumstances and hygiene, may be part of the treatment.

10. Preventing Accidents and Trauma:
Provide a secure habitat to avoid stress and harm to the shell. Hazards can include jagged objects, uneven surfaces, or spaces with insufficient hiding places. Reduce the possibility of mishaps in order to preserve shell integrity.

Detailed Grooming Procedure:
1. Observation and Evaluation:
Start by paying close attention to the shell of your box turtle. Keep an eye out for any indications of anomalies, discolorations, or modifications in the acute state. Make

a note of any locations that might need more examination.

2. Light Cleaning:

Use a gentle, moist cloth or sponge to gently wipe the shell's surface. Steer clear of abrasive objects and harsh chemicals since they can harm the keratin layer that protects the skin. Make sure there are no particles on the fabric that could scratch the shell.

3. soaking

Give your box turtle a basin of shallow water to soak in. In addition to providing hydration, soaking can soften any materials or detritus adhered to the shell. Let the turtle bath for fifteen to twenty minutes, making sure it feels safe throughout.

4. Cleaning (If Required):

A toothbrush with soft bristles can be used to remove tough dirt or algae. Concentrating on the areas where material has gathered, gently brush the shell. Aim for a soft, circular motion without using too much pressure.

5. Cleaning and Desiccation:

Rinse the turtle's shell with clean water to get rid of any leftovers after soaking and cleaning. Dry the shell with a gentle, spotless towel. Before putting the turtle back in its enclosure, make sure it is completely dry.

6. Hydrating Scutes in Shells:

After drying, you can apply a small layer of an oil or conditioner designed specifically for reptiles to preserve healthy scutes. This can keep the shell's natural shine and moisten the scutes. Refrain from overusing as too much application could draw debris.

7. UVB Radiation:

As directed by recommendations, place your box turtle in a location where it can get direct sunshine or make sure it has access to UVB lamps. The synthesis of vitamin D is increased by this exposure, which benefits calcium absorption and shell health.

8. Frequent visits to the vet:
Make time for routine veterinary examinations to guarantee your box turtle's general well-being. A vet with expertise in caring for reptiles can do comprehensive exams, provide dietary advice, and handle any new health issues.

Proactive Steps to Maintain Shell Health:
1. A well-rounded diet
Give your box turtle a diet that is well-balanced and covers all of its nutritional demands. To develop a nutrition plan customized to your turtle's age, species,

and overall health, speak with a veterinarian that specializes in reptiles.

2. Supplementing with Calcium:

Provide calcium supplements in accordance with a veterinarian's advice. The integrity and strength of the shell depend on calcium. Make sure the supplements are suitable for reptiles and adhere to the recommended dosage.

3. Sufficient Hydration:

Make sure the enclosure has a shallow water dish to help with optimum hydration. To promote consistent drinking and soaking habits, keep an eye on the cleanliness and quality of the water.

4. Ideal Enclosure Settings:

Provide the ideal enclosure conditions, with hiding places, suitable substrate, and a temperature gradient.

Reduce stresses like abrupt temperature swings and insufficient hiding places.

5. Enhancement of the Environment:

Enhance the natural environment to promote natural behaviors. Add features such as hiding places, spaces to bask, and items to explore. Participating in interesting activities promotes general wellbeing and brain stimulation.

6. Continual Cleaning Schedule:

Include a consistent cleaning schedule for the enclosure. Eliminate waste, leave food uneaten, and keep the substrate clean. To stop the emergence of shell problems, take immediate action to clean up any wet or unclean places.

7. Steer clear of Overhandling:

Box turtles may take some handling, but it's important to keep them as stress-free as possible. Steer clear of handling the turtle excessively, especially if it is sick or showing symptoms of discomfort.

8. Timely Veterinary Care:
Seek immediate veterinarian assistance if you notice any changes in the shell, behavior, or general health of your box turtle. In order to address possible difficulties, early detection and response are essential.

Typical Health Concerns and Solutions for Shells:
1. Pyramiding

- Problem: Pyramiding raises the scutes and is frequently linked to poor nutrition and dehydration.
- Intervention: Modify the diet to guarantee that the nutrients are properly balanced. Expand the

availability of pure water to stay hydrated. Speak with a veterinarian for specific advice.

2. Rotting Shells:

- Problem: Fungal or bacterial infections, such as shell rot, can cause soft areas, discolouration, or an unpleasant smell.

- Intervention: For diagnosis and treatment, speak with a veterinarian. It is possible to prescribe topical antifungal or antibacterial medicines. Boost living conditions and cleanliness.

3. Trauma or Damage:

- Problem: Mishaps or rough treatment might cause trauma or injury to the shell.

- Intervention: Create a secure atmosphere to reduce the possibility of accidents. In the event of an injury, get advice from a veterinarian regarding the best course of action and possible shell repair.

4. Anomalies:

Problem: Nutritional inadequacies, metabolic disorders, or environmental factors can cause shell malformations.

Intervention: To determine and treat the root causes, get advice from a veterinarian. Modify the food, enhance the surroundings, and heed veterinarian advice.

5. Excessive Scutes:

- Problem: Proliferating scutes might make it uncomfortable and prevent shell growth from normal.

- Intervention: Under veterinary supervision, carefully trim enlarged scutes using the proper instruments. Maintain a healthy diet and level of hydration to facilitate appropriate scute shedding.

In summary:

Responsible reptile care begins with grooming and keeping your box turtle's shell clean and healthy. You can support the general health of your turtle by being aware of their unique needs, giving them a balanced diet, making sure they stay hydrated, and giving them regular grooming. Frequent veterinary examinations, timely action when problems arise, and a dedication to providing an enriching habitat are all essential to keeping your box turtle friend's shell robust and alive. Your box turtle's bond will be strengthened as you go on this caring journey with them because of the time and effort you put into maintaining the health of their shell.

Chapter 9

The Box Turtle's Life Cycle: From Hatchling to Adulthood

A box turtle's life cycle is an amazing voyage with several developmental phases, each with its own set of obstacles, quirks, and turning points. To provide these fascinating reptiles the best care possible and to ensure their wellbeing, it is essential to comprehend their life cycle. We shall trace the amazing journey of a box turtle from the time of hatching to the time of its adulthood in this comprehensive investigation.

1. Stage of Egg:

Laying of Eggs and Nesting:

The box turtle's life cycle commences with the nesting and egg-laying stage. When building nests, female box turtles usually look for well-drained soil. It is common to see this activity in the spring or early summer. The female uses her hind limbs to dig a hole in which she delicately lays a clutch of eggs. Depending on the species, the number of eggs can vary but often falls between one and nine.

Time of Incubation:
The eggs go through a several-week-long incubation period once they are laid. Temperature and humidity are two examples of elements that affect how long an incubation takes. Shorter incubation times are typically the result of warmer temperatures. The eggs are allowed to grow and naturally hatch.

2. Phase of Hatching:
Coming Out of the Nest:
Hatchlings start to come out of the nest as the incubation period comes to an end. Temperature and brightness are two common environmental cues that

cause this emergence. To crack open the eggshell, hatchlings use an egg tooth, a tiny projection on the front of their upper jaw.

Challenges of Vulnerability and Survival:
At this point, hatchlings are very vulnerable. A few of the difficulties they encounter are predators, dangerous surroundings, and the requirement to locate good hiding places. Hatchlings of many box turtle species must rely on instinct and their own talents to navigate their surroundings because their parents provide little care.

3. Young Stage:
Expansion and Shell Development:
Hatchling box turtles go through the juvenile stage once they emerge from the egg. Their shells are malleable and fragile throughout this time, hardening as they grow. Healthy shell growth requires a good habitat, access to UVB sunshine, and adequate nutrients. With

time, the unique patterns on their shells become more noticeable.

Foraging and Shifting Diet:

Young box turtles aggressively search for a range of food sources, such as plant material, worms, snails, and tiny insects. As they become bigger, their diet changes, going from being mostly insectivorous to being omnivore and consisting of both plant- and animal-based meals.

Possibility of Predation:

During this phase, young box turtles are still susceptible to predators. They are vulnerable to a variety of predators, including as birds, animals, and other reptiles, due to their small size and flimsy shells. Locating appropriate hiding places becomes essential to their survival.

4. Stage of Subadult:

Sexual Differentiation and Maturity:

Box turtles go through sexual differentiation and maturity as they move through the sub-adult stage. Males and females can be distinguished from one another thanks to the increased visibility of sexual features. Female plastrons are flatter, and male plastrons tend to be larger and more concave.

Behavior and Dispersal of Territories:

Box turtles that are not yet adults may display territorial behavior, setting up home ranges and defending them. Certain individuals could start to spread out in pursuit of partners or appropriate environments. This phase represents a major turning point toward adulthood.

Sustaining expansion and shell development:

Box turtles continue to grow and their shells gradually harden during the sub-adult stage. For general health and to prevent shell abnormalities, adequate nourishment and access to appropriate environmental conditions are still necessary.

5. Adult Phase:

Mature Reproduction:

Reproductive maturity is what defines the adult stage. When they reach adulthood, box turtles can reproduce and take part in the yearly nesting ritual. Courtship displays are among the mating activities; males frequently pursue females and perform unique rituals to draw potential mates.

Nesting with the Cycle of Reproduction:

Reproductive cycles are followed by adult female box turtles, who look for appropriate nesting locations every year to lay clutches of eggs. Temperature and length of daylight are two environmental elements that frequently affect this behavior. During the breeding season, males vigorously search for females.

Determining Boundaries:

Box turtles that are adults mark off areas that they may protect from trespassers. Vocalizations, hostile posture, and head bobbing are examples of territorial behaviors. It's common for maintaining healthy populations to require enough space and habitat for several individuals.

Lifespan and Extended Life:

Some box turtles can live for several decades, making them well-known for their extended lifespans. A box turtle's lifespan is impacted by a number of variables, including genetics, environment, and human care quality. An extended and healthier life is a result of proper husbandry and routine veterinary care.

Elements Affecting the Life Cycle:

1. Conditions of the Environment:

For box turtles, temperature, humidity, and length of daylight are important factors at different phases of their life cycle. These environmental elements affect how birds build their nests, how long they incubate, and when their hatchlings emerge.

2. Quality of Habitat:

The box turtle's life cycle is greatly impacted by the habitat's quality. Box turtles at all stages benefit from a variety of substrates, clean water sources, appropriate nutrition, and access to hiding places.

3. Effect on Humans:

Box turtles are seriously threatened by human activity, which includes habitat destruction, pollution, and contact with automobiles and roads. Mitigating human impact requires conservation initiatives, habitat preservation, and ethical interactions with box turtles.

4. Challenges of Predation and Survival:

There are several types of predation that box turtles encounter during their life cycle. The survival of hatchlings, juveniles, and even sub-adults can be impacted by predators such raccoons, foxes, birds of prey, and snakes. Their survival depends in part on creating adequate hiding places and reducing the likelihood of predators.

5. Success in Reproduction:

The availability of suitable nesting sites, the availability of mates, and an individual's general health all affect reproductive success. Climate change, habitat fragmentation, and human activity can all have an impact on population dynamics and reproductive success.

Considering Conservation:

1. Preservation of Habitat:

The conservation of box turtles depends on the preservation of their natural habitats. Maintaining natural areas, reducing habitat loss, and establishing wildlife corridors all improve the general well-being of box turtle populations.

2. Highway Crossings and Death Rates:
Box turtles are seriously threatened by road mortality, particularly during the nesting and dispersal phases. Putting in place strategies like fencing, wildlife crossings, and public awareness campaigns can lessen the negative effects of roads on box turtle populations.

3. Programs for the Rehabilitation and Release of Wildlife:
Facilities dedicated to wildlife rehabilitation are essential to the care of box turtles that are hurt or lost. When appropriate, rehabilitation programs work to return

people to their natural environments so they can support wild populations.

4. Monitoring and Citizen Science:
Participating in citizen box turtle monitoring programs can yield important information about the health, distribution, and possible threats to the population. Initiatives in citizen science help to improve our knowledge of the ecology of box turtles and provide guidance for conservation efforts.

5. Outreach and Education:
Public education regarding the value of box turtles, their life cycle, and the difficulties they encounter is essential to their conservation. Outreach initiatives have the power to instill a sense of accountability and motivate behaviors that protect box turtle populations.

In summary:

The incredible journey of a box turtle's life cycle is characterized by adaptation, difficulties with survival, and reproductive techniques refined through evolution. Every stage demonstrates the tenacity of these fascinating reptiles, from the defenseless hatchling emerging from its egg to the territorial adult capable of passing on knowledge to the following generation. Humans, being environmental stewards, are essential to box turtle conservation. For box turtles to prosper in their natural habitats for many generations to come, responsible interactions, habitat preservation, and conservation efforts are crucial. We develop a greater respect for these unusual animals and the ecosystems they live in as we learn more about their life cycle.

Chapter 10

FAQs for Box Turtles: Answering Frequently Asked Questions and Myths

Box turtles are common companion reptiles because of their unique appearance and interesting habits. But they have special needs and considerations for care, just like any other pet. To provide correct information and encourage responsible ownership, we will address common questions and misconceptions about box turtles in this extensive guide.

1. Can You Pet Box Turtles?

Indeed, but with some caveats:

For those who are willing to devote the necessary time and energy to their upkeep, box turtles can make wonderful pets. It's important to realize, though, that they need particular surroundings, a balanced diet, and routine veterinary care. Box turtles have a long lifespan, and as they get older, their care requirements change, so potential owners should be ready for a long-term commitment.

2. Which Box Turtle Species Make Good Pets?

Popular Animals for Pets:

The Eastern Box Turtle (Terrapene carolina carolina) is one of the most common species of box turtle kept as pets. A number of other species are also kept in captivity, including the Ornate Box Turtle (Terrapene ornata), Gulf Coast Box Turtle (Terrapene carolina major), Three-Toed Box Turtle (Terrapene carolina triunguis), and Western Box Turtle (Terrapene ornata luteola). It is crucial to do your homework and select a species whose needs match your capacity to provide for them.

3. Is Ample Space Necessary for Box Turtles?

Indeed, They Need Enough Room:

Box turtles require a large, well-kept habitat in order to flourish. If housed indoors, the enclosure should be big enough to allow for exploration and have hiding places, a basking area, and the right substrate. An outdoor enclosure is ideal. The species and quantity of turtles will determine the enclosure's size. As long as it satisfies their unique needs, the larger, the better.

4. How Should My Box Turtle Be Fed?

A Diverse Diet is Essential:

Due to their omnivorous nature, box turtles should have a varied diet. Serve a variety of insects (like mealworms and crickets), worms, snails, leafy greens, and fruits. Supplements of calcium might be required, particularly for turtles kept in captivity. Regularly giving your dog or cat high-protein food can cause nutritional imbalances, so avoid doing so.

5. Can I house several box turtles in one enclosure?

Consideration Must Be Given Carefully:

Although some box turtles can live with other turtles, it is important to take special care when housing several turtles together. Territorial and aggressive behavior can happen, which can cause tension or harm. Enough room must be provided, hiding places must be found, and interactions must be observed. Be ready to split up turtles at any time if disputes emerge.

6. Do Box Turtles Require UVB Radiation?

UVB is indeed essential.

Box turtles need UVB light in order to synthesize vitamin D, which is essential for healthy calcium absorption and general wellbeing. Give them access to daylight or illuminate their enclosure with UVB light. Because UVB output decreases with time, make sure the light is changed out as recommended by the manufacturer.

7. Can I Frequently Handle My Box Turtle?

Minimal Handling Is Ideal:

Box turtles typically prefer little contact, though some may tolerate handling. They may become defensive or retreat into their shells as a result of being handled too much. To prevent damage, handle the animal carefully and support the plastron as well as the carapace when handling is required.

8. Is Water Required for Box Turtles to Swim?

Saturated Water Is Enough

Box turtles do not need deep water for swimming, but they do require access to shallow water for drinking and soaking. Provide a shallow dish that allows them to soak comfortably. Always ensure the water is clean and that they can easily enter and exit the dish.

9. Can Box Turtles Live Indoors?

Yes, with Proper Setup:

Box turtles can live indoors if provided with a suitable setup. Ensure the enclosure includes hiding spots, a basking area with UVB lighting, proper substrate, and a balanced diet. The enclosure's size should accommodate the turtle's need for exploration. Regular cleaning and maintenance are essential for indoor habitats.

10. Do Box Turtles Hibernate?

Yes, Some Species Hibernate:

Many box turtle species undergo a period of brumation, which is similar to hibernation. During this time, their metabolic rate decreases, and they become less active. The need for hibernation varies among species, and not all box turtles hibernate. Mimicking natural seasonal changes is important for those that do.

11. How Can I Tell the Gender of My Box Turtle?

Physical Characteristics Differ:

Determining the gender of a box turtle involves examining physical characteristics. In general, males often have larger and more concave plastrons, longer and thicker tails, and may exhibit more colorful markings. Females typically have flatter plastrons and shorter, slimmer tails.

12. Do Box Turtles Carry Salmonella?

Caution is Advised:

Like many reptiles, box turtles can carry Salmonella bacteria. It's essential to practice good hygiene when handling them. Wash hands thoroughly after any interaction, and avoid contact with their habitat or water. Be cautious, especially when around young children, elderly individuals, or those with compromised immune systems.

13. What Is Pyramiding in Box Turtles?

Shell Deformity from Improper Care:

Pyramiding is a shell deformity characterized by raised scutes. It often occurs due to improper diet and hydration during a turtle's early years. Feeding a well-balanced diet, providing access to clean water, and ensuring proper humidity levels can help prevent pyramiding.

14. Can I Release a Captive Box Turtle Into the Wild?

Releasing Captive Turtles is Not Advised:

Releasing captive box turtles into the wild is generally not advised. Captive turtles may transmit diseases that might damage wild populations, and they may lack the critical abilities for survival. Additionally, releasing them without adequate consideration of local legislation can have legal ramifications.

15. How Long Do Box Turtles Live?

Long Lifespan:

Box turtles are recognized for their longevity. In captivity, they can survive for several decades, with some individuals reaching 50 years or more. Providing correct care, diet, and frequent veterinarian check-ups contribute to their general health and lifespan.

16. Are Box Turtles Nocturnal?

Diurnal with Some Variation:

Box turtles are generally diurnal, meaning they are active during the day. However, there can be variances among individuals and species. Some may become more active between dawn and dusk, while others may show more nocturnal characteristics. Providing a constant light-dark cycle in captivity helps manage their activity.

17. Do Box Turtles Shed Their Shells?

No, Shells Do Not Shed:

Contrary to widespread notions, box turtle shells do not shed. The scutes on their shells may naturally wear down and be replaced over time, but the complete shell does not shed like the skin of some reptiles.

18. Can I Use Sand as Substrate for My Box Turtle?

Use Caution with Sand:

While sand may be used as part of the substrate, it's vital to be cautious. Fine sand can be eaten, leading to impaction, a potentially dangerous condition. Mixing sand with different substrates like coconut coir or cypress mulch can produce a more suitable habitat.

19. Are Box Turtles Aggressive?

Territorial Behaviors May Occur:

Box turtles can demonstrate territorial characteristics, especially during the breeding season. While they are not normally hostile, disputes can emerge if numerous turtles are kept together in limited area. Providing appropriate hiding locations and monitoring their activity is vital.

20. Can I Paint My Box Turtle's Shell?

Absolutely Not Advised:

Painting a box turtle's shell is severely discouraged. The shell is a key element of their structure, and any compounds given to it can be damaging. Paint can cause health problems by preventing vital UVB absorption. Never put their natural well-being ahead of artistic tastes.

In summary:

It is essential to comprehend the requirements and traits of box turtles in order to give them the right care and build a strong bond with these fascinating reptiles. We enable both new and existing owners to make decisions that promote the health and wellbeing of their box turtle companions by clearing up common misconceptions and responding to frequently asked concerns. It is possible to guarantee a happy and enriching experience for both humans and box turtles by practicing responsible ownership in conjunction with a dedication to continuous learning and adaptation.